Playtime

Flood Editions, Chicago

William Fuller
Playtime

Published by Flood Editions

www.floodeditions.com

ISBN 978-0-9903407-3-7

Design and composition by Quemadura

Printed on acid-free, recycled paper

in the United States of America

This book was made possible in part

through a grant from the Illinois Arts Council

Some of these poems have appeared in

Chicago Review, *The Claudius App*,

A Fiery Flying Roule, *Houseguest*, *Infinite
Editions*, *Jubilat*, *Kenyon Review Online*,

No Prizes, *SNOW*, and *Sous Les Pavés*.

fforget not yet . . .

I

I

Witchcraft

After being possessed and overcome by the Devil I lost access
to my own thoughts. This meant that in order to recover them
I had to ask question after question of strangers, which for the
most part they couldn't answer. When someone felt he or she
could answer, I took careful note of what was said and how it
was said, and made a point to request an account of its origin and
development. In this way, over many months and years, I was
slowly able to regain access to my mental life, even translating
it into propositions for public or private use. But problems soon
arose when my intentions proved too elusive for my means to
convey them, which resulted in unexpected deflections and dis-
tortions, and turned my ideas into twigs. Despite this I have
something to tell you. What for so long you and I have observed
together, day in and day out, has been constantly modified by
what we don't see, leaving one whole side of experience blank.
And now that we've grown old, we lack energy to work out
what these dark lanes or vacant areas impart to us. Although the
intellect takes pleasure in exercising itself according to the five-
fold method—listening, reading, grasping, remembering, forget-
ting—there are some tasks that make it bristle. I hereby repre-
sent myself to you as the residue of things that aren't true. Or
can these even be distinguished? Whose face shades the differ-
ence? Whose memory stores it?

Horror Rage and
Pallid Exasperation

I can't really worry about what this says or doesn't say. To begin
with, our village has just imploded. All that remain are things
not endowed with properties—certainly not enough to call them
things. On another day a more generous analysis might point to
the role these could still play in our sustenance, and how their
sensed presence might actuate our seeking them out. Attempts
could be made to arrange them mentally, and perhaps even phys-
ically if one imagines their arrangement to occupy something
other than mental space—assuming the latter isn't also physical
space—and in that condition they start to repel one another and
eventually start to repel themselves, as the absence of proper-
ties yields a kind of free-for-all with no apparent logic or pur-
pose. Nevertheless these movements urge us to observe. The
more intently we study them, the more we seem to absorb their
indeterminate character, bringing us into alignment with them,
as though ceasing to be intelligible to ourselves and to others
were a shared feature, a form of community, an objective world.
If we could simply pause and ponder this we might come to lead
normal lives—if normal signifies a kind of transcendence, or
state beyond discernment and distinction, a grove, as it were,
bordered by rocks jutting into the sun, which we stumble across
in pursuit of some sister spirit, or lured on by the absence of cur-
tains and the distant presence of trees.

Old Fuller Burying Ground

one escapes what one believes through
indistinct cognition of empty
flows, blocking indifference
to dead voices, raising each pitch

by a process called earth-gazing
enough to sate a seeker's sight
but choosing only those ripe
for incorporeal contact or abstract

participation in the knowledge
of what they really are, never
more alike than when shown
poring over every eye in town

interchangeable but not identical
while the heat rolls off them
returning to a state upon which
intelligence is consequent

Hampton

I lay in a field in eastern Connecticut, surrounded by my long-dead ancestors, who had arrived there from Salem Village at the end of the seventeenth century. Each full moon we would lean back on elbows and attempt to converse. Over time something like friendship arose among us, even though it would not be an exaggeration to say that during our most lucid nights we only understood every tenth word that was spoken. From these words, however, we were able to prepare sentence-like statements whose significance we would painstakingly try to convey, although these explanations contained large gaps, making them more impenetrable than what they were meant to explain. As years passed it grew apparent that fewer and fewer words were being understood, so that a full night's discourse of ten thousand utterances might be distilled into "Love's lowest souls are goats" or "Seas Woods Trees." Sometimes the long night would yield exactly one intelligible word; other times, despite surges of vocal sound, not a single distinct syllable could be deciphered. Rather than discourage us, these baffling exchanges drew us more warmly together, under the bright moon, in the twisted vegetation. So much so that one spring night we succeeded in piecing together—God knows how—the phrase "Subdimensional projection"—which was then followed by years of silence. Twelve nights ago that silence was finally broken as the moon rose in its *Circuit, Course, and Backward Course* and four of us spontaneously announced, "Nothing is future in reference to now."

6

¶

This is a true story. "You know miserably little," the fox told the king. The king took umbrage and killed the fox, then sat down to read his prospectus. That night the fox came back to life and spoke *beautiful expressions full of beautiful conjunctions and lovely disjunctions*, which the king heard through the walls of his dream. But what was the basis of this hearing? And why was the fox permitted thus to speak? Were those assigned to examine the situation familiar with the techniques the fox employed? We who had trusted the fox were not consoled when he publicly repudiated his "difficult, dark, hard, strange, harsh, and almost unheard-of words." For even as these hung dripping on the fence, new fences were being built, as well as extensive gardens, and itineraries were being planned for crossing the seas to announce the sun.

¶¶

My experiments at first yield meager fruit. There is shouting and revising and moralizing. By nightfall there are ten elephants stationed along the edge of the square, while opposite them a thousand searchers have anxiously gathered. From atop the elephants, tall scarecrows watch. They are tempted to note patterns in the scene below, but its aspects are so various and the names to be applied to them so few that nothing can be described save the scarecrows' own presence as the crucible of perception. What should we be calling this? What do others want it to be called? A sign depicts a house whose roof has been torn off by an unseen giant. Another sign shows a headless horse rearing up on its hind legs. The words *house* and *horse* begin to circulate through the square—slowly at first, then rapidly, until at length they fling themselves back and forth like flames, cut by an occasional cry, not of distress but of amazement, as the sedentary and the solitary take flight.

Kings

The chances are good you were built from kings like these, whoever you are, so it's no wonder they're inside you banging to get out and then regretting it immediately when they do—and I've come up from the basement with a stack of leaves and a bent candle, intending to set new rules for accepting appointments, although not today as I fall back on absolutely no resources, and even the kings are sleeping or at most paying attention to nothing but the garden's gradual self-augmentation. Over time they grow old, die, are buried, to rise again with green eyes, plant flowers, negotiate contracts, advocate secular liberation, seek repeal of Section 2 (a), and become comfortable with activities that are increasingly hard to define.

The Inhabitants

In responding to the issue I wanted to take time to revolve in my mind all the possibilities of response, in all their various hues and shades, not preferring one response over another until I had cycled through every variation I could think of, even if it took months, which it did. At the end of the process I had more or less settled on an approach to take, an approach that required two or three tools to put into practice, tools not easy to obtain, I learned, given that by the beginning of the last century they had become obsolete, and in fact some suggest that such tools may only have existed in books. So I dismissed the entire matter and pretended by that act to have completed my task. Needless to say, this was rejected out of hand, not by the powers that be, but by me, shunted off as I was onto a siding, and hoping to avoid all metaphors in characterizing my divided state, which I managed to accomplish by closing my eyes, pointing my face toward the earth, and dropping silently to my knees. The mental pictures I saw then are difficult to describe, but the way they floated across the surface of my brain as I followed their ramifications in and among certain wax figures seemed the result of an arcane and beautiful calculation, a calculation that determined not only the consistency of all phenomena inside this realm, but also underlay the curious pattern of rents or fissures in its general fabric, through which one occasionally caught sight of concepts shaped like animals, both wild and domestic, including several small dogs and a fox, each waiting to be modified pursuant to a series of not-quite-knowable side agreements. It turns out that I would later obtain one such agreement. As a result I am now convinced there *was* an issue I should have responded to, if not the one I thought; in fact, it seems there were quite a number of issues, all of them unknown to the Inhabitants, who were judged too peripheral to be consulted, despite their presence alone bestowing on the place whatever reality it possessed. So year after year while the Inhabitants struggled to make themselves conspicuous, their efforts were seen as only compounding a problem cut deep into the innermost ring of general anxiety, a problem whose solution came to be envisaged in terms of a claim, and on that basis all doubt was set aside and remedies were sought.

Delaware

As I was dropping off to sleep a pair of peacocks stepped out of the book I was reading and poked cautiously through the room. At the same time I received notice that all thick words were to be sent to Delaware. The notice came by order of someone who needn't give reasons for what he does, and if asked for one would simply turn himself into a tree. Days grew longer and became more involved, twining around each other and starting to climb the stairs, while those for whom the days served as proxies found no efficacy in this. Yet there was merit in letting the situation ride itself out, for its key elements were as furtive as peacocks and had shrewdly performed acts whose consequences would only be discovered weeks, months, decades later—and why not—if nothing else was to become of them, for beyond them lies nothing to be comprehended. Gradually a large idea began to divide itself into smaller sections or panels, which fell naturally into two broad groups—it was of great interest to note a rivalry developing between these groups as they both rose skyward. And the sky held them in tension. Who would want to modify this charged state, which hungered for its own undoing, perhaps leading the way at last to a distant, more sympathetic jurisdiction?

The words came back washed in gold.

The Parks

At the eternal prospect, eyed closely, we close our eyes and lift a city block high in the air with nothing falling off, then set it back down to oceanic noise as amber fluid leaks back from yesterday and the shapeless gather round, like constellated litter. The sun presents itself as gracious agent of anomalous illumination or figure transcribed from dark sources regulating the east, in whose light nothing is lost save incriminating memoranda, which leave word where to find them should dispossession bury all and they prove useful, although at that point who would know. *[If you accept this you've agreed to be governed by the kind of reasoning that asks you simply to sit still for a moment and peer into the sand-colored vagueness, foregoing its appraisal in any but proprietary terms, which climb perpendicular to the empyrean, spreading over the backs of those whose devotion to its arched aura grows deeper and deeper from continuous recital of facts forced out of their sockets by the gleam or glimmer of spots unknown—our parks are full of them.]*

Ahmed Sabit

Who did not do the thing that they had done, to render last first and impart a glow to it, which it lacked—still lacks. Everywhere words oppose how breathless tender footplate was, had it not existed or had risen from soulless habitation like Abednego, to whose forest sleep clings. No mention that nothing is accomplished absent the model, otherwise not true, but its truth endows visionary parts. So help me that night they came jostling to truth's house, seeking a release. My opinion is they could have gotten one had they restrained themselves—for the abrupt sinless hexagon was transparent consideration. To manipulate the throttle is to engage the event, and to look ahead is to hasten toward a terminus, buying time while others sort through bins, inasmuch as they would like to fulfill requirements without using the blood of fellow creatures.

Anoesis

There are within an ambit of circumstance certain principles that attach themselves to the agents or actors for whom our daily shifting scenes appear to have been arranged, and who, while existing only within those scenes, are neither contained by them nor detached from them, but hover among and between while time unfolds in whatever sequence is elected, if by *elected* one means the unalloyed application of indifferent forms reverting to their more general, less numerous, prototypes, pacing back and forth in the distance, and challenging all to carry out acts consistent with the structure they maintain. Whether I knew this then or know this now isn't important. For words drip like wax, and while there may be a need to extend them over a rough surface, similar to the one immediately to my right, I prefer what may happen in other regions, with other agents or actors, who might overcome their own weaknesses in order to insert themselves irrevocably into what they see and hear, and enjoy a plausible form of life that cuts away everything, enticing fresh sounds from above.

The Unicorn

The system slows down for me to catch up and I'm almost there, stepping quickly through the bushes and taking note of objects on the periphery not worth enumerating, then climbing a small hill to the narrow bridge despite my inability either to move an inch or know where I'm going—when all of a sudden I sink into the earth to the sound of underground breezes stretching themselves over escarpments and galleries, and I release my thoughts into the majority view that there is only *coolness*. But intensities gather just below the level at which I can detect them. Under normal circumstances I would be able to tell from the behavior of the crows perched in the corner of the grove, and their messages back and forth, whether the day had reached a real depth of excitement. From here, though, nothing is visible, except a trail of sleeping roots. The roots are not unrelated to the lack of confidence I feel as I gather in what light I can. The underground sky is black with patches of brown and looks to be five feet wide. The air within it carries a certain luster that hardens at the edge. After an hour or two a flock of splendid thoughts arrives, kindling responsive sparks before everything clouds up. Then a small river tunnels through my eyes.

El Perro con Botas

Does mist form in reaction to what you dream? I will use whatever I have learned to attack this question, but first I want to sit here and watch the future arrive from the past, or from what precedes the past, make a clearing for it, build it a fire &c., and in this space speak words or things similar to words—homonyms, paronyms, heteronyms, tautonyms—all without moving lips and without thinking any thought not devoted to complete repose. At length my awareness dilates into a broad sea upon which tall towers appear to float. Between the towers wires are strung, from which hundreds of rags hang, the whole scene waving up and down with the motion of the water. As I drift back, the towers shrink and multiply, turning into frozen stalks on dry land, while the rags clump into brittle burrs that cling to me as I weave through them on my way to the road. It is early evening. Snow has begun to fall although there are no clouds. Rather than question this, I start to make notes, then sit down to analyze them in case I am asked to hazard a guess as to the situation's overall value. I have an expectation that others with similar experience and training to mine will consider these comments useful, if not embrace them, although I have come too far to trust to this, and so have built a series of doors through which my findings can exit and enter at will, depending on the conditions that develop and the assumptions governing them. While I know there is no one answer, I hope to establish that if there *were* such an answer it would fall within a range one could calculate. Then I wonder, am I in a place where all the links are broken, although they seem to be completely intact? To be rational is to affix one's desire to the geese overhead, throbbing like bass clarinets; to be irrational is to close one's ears to them, spinning counterclockwise as they pivot off the air. Soon the rising moon discloses a small dog, whose nearby presence calms me, that is until it speaks. A train rumbles in the distance, setting the dog's teeth on edge. Headlights wind up a steep hill that has imposed itself out of nowhere. I sense the pulses of animals all around me; I know the contents of their minds. Yet so can anyone else.* Where was the road before it came to exist here, sliding through the dark? What arises from it perpetually? I take the medicine of negation and exchange weariness for emptiness. I recall Peter Sterry's phrase, "A poet on a clear night surprised by thieves."

But now it is bright day. The dog sleeps. On the next ridge two foxes sourly calculate their pensions, then navigate a path into the trees. Behind them ten thousand poets assume human form, which one should not confuse with being. Everything else is compressed into a dot called the sun.

---

* For a reported cost of around $400,000.

Massillon to Gambier

horse-drawn glare
ushers faintly

2

Mhous

my brains are a wilderness
but they observe courtesies
like you do both specified and
unspecified on the third of May last

I listen to them over and over
and without question one of
the strangest beings I have
ever known has emerged from them

will their light be obscured when
the upper limit makes them cohere
poets philosophers mathematicians
shall in those flames be transfigured

my heart is a scarecrow of fresh
green leaves and flesh standing
in the sun—watch as fingers go
numb from its defilements

Tomorrow Afternoon

No one plays a predominant role, nothing special is attached to anyone's perspective to give edge or advantage, each has a set of observations to supply, and each observation complements, exactly, every other. We sit around a table while a notebook circulates. Inside the notebook are sketches of people swimming lazily out to the margins and back again. Occasionally the margins disappear, which confuses all of us, but especially the swimmers, who find themselves having gone far beyond their former limit, although they somehow feel encouraged to proceed. Soon they are swimming off the page and into the room, and then through the walls and into the courtyard, where employees gather on benches to watch. At length they cross the boundary into night and swim through darkened towns while doctrines form in their wake, and the doctrines are taught, and questions are posed of the teachers, who are ranked on a scale of one to ten for their ability to abstract themselves from the sensorium.

Morpheus

I went to a place where nothing happened whose effects could not be felt elsewhere—a place for the sleepers and a place for those too rested to sleep. Then my car fell off the mountain—it's one of those things I can't explain. After midnight music rose like steam, obscuring the way, but cleansing it as well. And beyond, in the forest next to the vacant lot, a bird made a noise like a bat. Whatever the planets were doing was of no interest to me. Many wore halos of contamination. Most were treading water of some sort.

New Jugband Blues

They were not in a position to disclose what they knew
only that someone had traveled there to meet with them
and had brought a piece of writing
designed to remove any impediment to
their understanding the situation they were in—
that is intractable soil as De Quincey would say
for there was a feeling among them
that they were alone in thinking
that they were alone
although were we to catch up with them later
we would learn that nothing had happened yet—
but a decision's clearly been made—and
there are one or two thoughts
still to wring from this
even as Hesperus entreats us
to perform other activities
pursuant to nightfall
which calms every molecule
if one has placed the senses
in their proper order
to receive the incoming entity
as Plotinus would say—
otherwise who would consider this
even a nominal possibility?

From My Windows

I left the old granary for an extended trip and the rain fell and I was soaked through but continued vaguely to progress day after day, until at length I found another granary next to which people were transacting business unconnected with grain. Beneath the trees I saw musicians manipulating their instruments as if they were milking cows, and every so often the whole scene would suddenly lurch forward. I considered making a comment, but then noticed everything on the surface of the earth had become completely silent. At that point they—who they were I couldn't tell—approached me from behind and took away the god I was traveling with. And of course I was upset but this was all pantomime so I swallowed my protests. They kept the god for ten days as a guarantee, while according to regulation I was made to scrub the path with sticks and sprinkle it with oil. Each night I withdrew to a small ditch by an olive grove. In due course the god and I were sent back to the place that had ransomed us, even as we had abandoned it, and without uttering any sound we leapt together from the second to the third tier deep inside the predicament we held true to, and this was noted by others.

Octomore

They made the same argument but without much energy or conviction so it was hard for anyone who hadn't spent months with them to know what it meant to them and how serious they were about what they were saying. Instead people turned their attentions elsewhere, most of them pressing their noses to the window to watch as a small herd of deer crossed the lawn obviously looking for something, which led to conjecture about what that could be and could its nature be divined from their behavior, or for that matter could the nature of the deer be divined from the gazes directed out the window and the activity of the minds assessing what was beheld there—this was *my* question, given that I couldn't see any of this from where I was sitting but relied on an oral description provided by someone leaning his back up against the window and viewing the scene solely by means of a small mirror mounted on the opposite wall. I listened on the other side of this wall, where you sat with me, offering your own commentary while firmly guiding my arm back into the socket.

The Master Science

All over the system that sort of work was considered useful, if not overwhelmingly so—divided between the wilderness and the great towns, within which a discipline would circulate, and an antipathy to sin set in, holding temptation in one hand while placing the inclination to yield to it in the other, balancing both against a deep respect for smooth textures. The silver light diverted one's eyes into the exact rut cut by forebears through the milky undergrowth, the path to sacrifice. To notice these things was to exercise judgment without intending to because they were not there to be noticed, but stayed apart in a world we didn't inhabit, a world whose creatures were unaware of them, although had they been so they would not have been fazed, even if such awareness rose well above the minimum standard. And in the freezing light of their sun what difference would it have made for someone *not* to have been oblivious? The last and final revolution eliminated all work so it never came up. But that led to fresh problems in terms of dogma, which is where we are now.

The Electric Garden

I grow tired of trying to understand why they think that way, or even if what they are doing should be called thinking, given that it concludes in a low buzzing sound interspersed with clicks. I decide to ignore them in favor of the electric garden. The waterfall is bright blue; the rocks are dark yellow; the shrubs are black and white. You are standing in the midst of these and you look happy, although your size is out of proportion to everything else, so I'm beginning to think you might be a statue. Overhead the planets creep in close and stream their influences. This causes the garden to pitch back and forth, as each influence takes its turn prevailing. The sky cuts the air into unequal parts, anointing my opportunity to withdraw. And while I'd like to know if that's really appropriate here, depending on whether duties are altered, and also on what role bifurcation might play, there's no time—Saturn is pouring down.

The Vole

We made a wide right turn onto the road, breathing loudly, although not at the macrocosmic level. We were preoccupied with a certain claim asserted by vegetable life, and by a sign. It never occurred to us to be more circumspect, less obtrusive, or that we were highly fortunate to be able to speak our minds at the exact moment their contents became organized enough to be spoken. We might have known, as indeed we do now, that these contents were so relentlessly and excessively detailed that to articulate them to any but the most sympathetic audience would be a serious mistake, one which could cost us years of concentrated effort to win back our authority. Nonetheless, we possessed shape and motion, and propelled ourselves forward day after day until our momentum was finally persuaded to associate itself with more restrained impulses, tending to rest. And in this state, with its extra features, we came to know thoughtless things and learned how to unthink them, in exchange for a payment.

The Sphere

Parts of me have just come loose. I am annoyed because I don't know exactly which parts they are or what roles they play in keeping me together. The sun has dimmed, or else there is a kind of haze slowly obscuring it. At the same time objects look brighter—cars, trees, fences, and my corresponding ideas of them, are all brighter. I see a green fringe everywhere, like a giant margin. Everything is retreating to this margin to plan the next move. Certain principles begin to emerge but I can't quite grasp them—they bring to mind blank maps of nameless places that hold one's interest owing to their odd shapes. In some of these places I hope to find material for use in other spheres. Of course the word *sphere* comprises many different kinds of spheres, including this sphere, which seems to be an animal (in whatever sense that should be taken).

Nottamun Town

the most extraordinary
animal approached
holding out
enormous hands

then late last night
became extinct
vanishing through
a slit of sky

while earth slept
and melons and figs
went unperceived
or were split open

and an unborn
widow emerged
bearing the remote
but theoretically

feasible prospect
that her emulated brain
would one day comprise
all ten perfections

shot through with
shining splendors
traveling at
incredible speed

toward a pair of naked feet
in a river
binding all that fluctuates
to a little flesh

made cunningly
its transpontine
calm a-shiver
and without access to tools

that would expose
its leaking heart—
I may not live
to reach a truth

whose drift
I find discouraging
this hat for example
was the last one he wore

and now he's cleaning
the buttery floor
in the pure flame
of early sun

billowing out
like a cloud
on which
an image is drawn

or out of which
things cohere
waves of people
not looking up

then one day
there's no atmosphere
only white ink
and residuum of trees

or else something inconceivably
complicated not
its transparent
reduction

near the end of a great pier
stretching into space—
space that can be decanted
into other space

if its rigidity
won't moderate—
what happened last
should have happened first

what happened first
should have happened last
but what is venerable
happens first and last—

there is nothing in this cup
although I can taste it
out of ten claims
not one is true

Ali Baba

On a cool morning with rain about to fall, someone walks by on the way to the station. There's a secret error in the scene, which is in a perpetual state of flux. What is needed is always being replaced, following the plan repeatedly submitted. Nine simple figures appear to float in reference to this plan, their values increasing as they tend toward an ideal existence "not subservient to practice." Notes are taken to prepare for what comes next— clearly a call to account for something, for a change in strategy, or an attempt to revive vintage ambitions, which slip behind the glass in an effort to conceal themselves, or defer their full presence until the last depth has been sounded and the sky wakes upside down. They remain idiosyncratic to the end of time, when all will finally have conformed to them in the strict sense. The strange disturbances up on the ridge are unrelated.

For Josky

I drained the can, poked holes in the sides with an awl, filled it up with seeds and stones, and shook it in time to the music. When the music stopped something unfamiliar took its place. On the way home I was approached by a man carrying a lengthy, detailed description of a new and dynamic system. I was fascinated by this but too timid to question him, which he took as an invitation to speak: "I apply negative skill to a quantity indistinguishable from zero, and Peter reminds me I'm simply making noise. For all the elements of our enterprise were long ago made available to us, on the assumption that we had the energy and determination to complete it, which we claimed we did have, for better or for worse. Over the years hundreds have come and gone and it lies beyond my scope to describe the circumstances of their arrivals and departures, or the intricate arguments dreamed up to show that all changes had been foreseen and accounted for. So with Peter standing by in the name of objectivity, I transport factors from the past into the present, while the future exhibits a contempt too heartfelt to offend." I kept on walking and eventually came to a stream that ran along the base of a saffron-colored wall. There were empty beings floating in the stream; they had human faces but their bodies were difficult to see. Perhaps one of them was the straw man I'd been looking for.

Funky New Bell

Today you cannot do without what makes you walk through a field of pernicious concepts to a garden of beautiful exempla. In the center of the garden is a fountain, next to which is a screen where every detail of your life has been arranged, each with its own heading. Along the edges of the screen small faces appear and disappear, some of them apparently associated with aspects of your behavior, others not, or at least that's the impression one gets. After staring at these you wonder whether this is meant to be a game—a rendezvous of old events and tendencies waiting to be appraised and reconciled, or combined into new forms representing you at all possible stages. How often have your versions come here? You check the items on the screen for accuracy, and correct them where required. In response to what you're doing the faces become animated, some smiling, some grimacing. One of the faces, you're told, is that of Queen Mab herself, putting the whole episode into a different light. Her expression is blank and does not change in the slightest despite your efforts to force her to acknowledge you. Regardless, you've become completely engaged and active, marking, changing, clicking, saving, refreshing, until all your specifications are met, thanks to your intimate and comprehensive knowledge of the subject. You close your eyes and lean back into the black air as it swells.

Glidepath

How could you ask what is a classical education without sylla-
bles to make you attentive to the heart of a word or set of in-
tensities burning to make you aware how desperate we are for
water and something to accompany it after diligent search of re-
membered events divided up among us that turned out to be the
same event taking place then and now and to come, with smooth
edges, so to speak, so smooth they decline to zero before any
voice can sum them up or anticipate the next significant oscil-
lation. The slope of night adjusts toward day, waking the trem-
ulous disc. The spirit of what can happen has changed into
the flesh of what *has* happened, and we make room for it. I have
you who have me. I am standing with you but apart. What is
the plan.

Future Interests

The molecules turned tenderly toward me while a fist gathered speed. The dark sky's core glowed—its radiance was less than a boundless or immeasurable radiance, but more than a practical, literary, or mechanical radiance. The unshaped stars exceeded all refinement, passing from peak to peak inside a tractable sphere. The trees chanted elegant lightning through the wet leaves of outer space. The glorious morning lay dead asleep and the thought of waking it likewise slept. Our then living descendants had not yet been born.

3

Chagrin

I went down to the place where I was and I wasn't there. I had formed a new perspective between the water and the trees. The wind had folded me up, though I'd forgotten it or had assigned the memory to someone else, someone whose name is missing from my account, who sleeps under the earth and wakes inside the sky, on the day and hour of Mercury, the moon decreasing out of time.

As ever, we were then.

Playthyme

Not here in the asylum fire where it's nice to carry chains. Nor chains for these clinging to fences built to enclose those in service to these. Nor some minimum level of integrity to assure that they can be told apart or kept straight. Here they are. Nor what they will be stripped of when banners arrive to unglue them. They wander in, all nice to have and never struggle with sumptuary cares. I know exactly why they want it like that— so that no one can tell them what to do when they get here, especially after they refuse to leave. I once saw them rejecting paronymous pleas, trying different keys, morbidly groping. They lacked conviction. Whereas our happy pair parse their own themes and their talk recalls the pale paintings that used to hang in the hall, although they're off to a rough start, lacking a standard agenda. (This plenary obstacle rears up, plucks its own fur, and displays a temperament no one really has.*) Make peace still, they tell me, sweep your room clean. It *would* have been nice to have, the dawn. The cowbells would have rung all night. I turn to the fire in the membrane, escalating through language. In some respects the spirit was dislodged the moment your soft nod acknowledged it. We are the difference, you or I said. There must be changes inside our skulls in order for this to

---

* Of inveterate consideration is a supportive construction consistent with the highest intermediate value ascribed to intentional, unconscionable, and egregious conduct, whose features drain themselves of any color not red.

take. There must be changes without regard to any conflict. So why did you? *I* wouldn't, and now I, formerly known as me, quite forget my name and sit here gazing at it. I will be the first to die, out of selflessness, drying up the fields in advance of one last task. Although I'm not destitute of means to undertake that task, I'm insufficiently plastic to embrace all of its subsidiary parts. Meanwhile this page just shakes its head and says, "Mind the boundaries for what they are. Defer to the naked word, contradictory and absurd. These situations are almost always equivocal."

Playtime

I can still see him
but won't indulge
the urge to look

is that a leaf
or his voice
sounding terrified

or a door
which opens
on an act

imparticipable
from the neck down
shattered

by opportunities
to exploit
what I never saw

or thought
I never found
the mice

the flies
the triggered
depths

smoldering
noiselessly
you'd call it

stillness
the stillness
of One among ones

gathered in a mirror
or pledged against
some random

commitment
out of which
a center is assigned

made conspicuous
by its habit
of staring

which is part
of its nature
while its antecedent nature

cautiously
follows
it around

do you think
this place
with its headlands

would be inclined
to rotate
within the visible wheel

the vacuum
upheld by
homunculi

they are not
present
but also are not

gone
the creditor
has asked me

to hold off
sorceries—
may the mountain

keep you back
five lines
erased

the most
spectral
part involves

a front yard
with rabbits
one by one

the hawks
rise in billows
pear-shaped

frost no sooner
clings to
ground

than fingertips
tilt toward
Mars

thinnest zone
under this
canopy

a state
reached by ladder
a lull

before
stalling out
in a passageway

its *intractable*
*magi*c
disguised

as something
carefully
reproduced

how do they
make these coils
the crows

have a question
the hemisphere
moves back

the temples
traditionally
catch fire

in the fog
each upright
tone

conjures
its own level
than which

can be said
nothing more
than *adieu* effect

ruffling
wave-like
forms

to soak paths
or thread
them like snakes

lucid
and strange
flinging

cracked
concrete
sandwiches

at various
personnel
roaming

the momentary
calm
no breath

can quantify
that candle
in the dark

the teares shall
wash away
the foundations

of their houses
at noon
no shadows

spring
to telegraph
uncertainty

amazed there
is us
in readiness

tainted
with radiance
tented with snow

ears nose eyes
still warm
therefore must

feast
fascinated
that nickel

grinds uphill
while I watch
a flock

of frozen folk
unfold
although

they do not exist
despite
ascetics' claims

somebody
taps the glass
volatile

peaks of
shadows
blaze

curious
crust
remains

crystynde
nightfall
seedlings

dry out
at the bar
nervous

signs squint
facing forward
for now

emptiness
swells up
to speak

don't stop
consolidating
your pains

slightly
elevated
before death

preposterous exit
looms
a complete blank

always and ever
we stood where
we weren't—

no one was—
puns
don't argue

sowing
salt
in syrup

whiff
of meal
lingers

but we would
not stay
who are

not here
in the air
waiting

out of
loving kindness
with solemn

sound how
deep
the tree

reaches up
to bat
the sun

but now
it's gone
no wires

to maintain
the way
moonbeams

open-ended
which one
that one

not dead
until now
clumps

feet up
feel
it's

so
so feel it
all the next day

drags
here
for repair

no one ordered
those lights
a drudge

next door
is endpoint
of resistance

the
guru
analytical

drips
incompetence
then appears to faint

the numbers
shout
conquering lion

in twos
and threes
reinforced

handwriting
sinks into
brown fields

the dynamic
one pager
is called

On Voidness
or
neurosis

disguised
as principle
how is it born

o master nothing
ambrosial
produced

no possibility
unforeseen
moors it

with chutes
swinging slowly
through the dark

those who don't
shiver
don't know

which universe
has been applied
the icy

pavement
counsels
rise above

near the end
of Book Two
us

on whom
it dawns
clearly

see
what the
problem is

till one
greater
observes

and being
smart
concludes

without disappointment
it can't
happen

here
under our mutilated
alphabet—

we're not wrong
to persist
in natural explanations

absent
adequate
security

use ointment
next time
whether

a dream
or a joke
what

exactly is
streaming
offshore

on the twenty-first
that's you
I suppose

knowing
whose blood
drives compromise

elsewhere
ineffable
isolation

or barbarism
fitted with
screens

standard
headlight
code

unreadable
without
pinching

bodies
into rivers
regarde

inchanted glass
whose reflection
binds

regions
which
produce pain

we don't
actually
go inside

but stand off
to the left
snow falls

we move nearer
are there lights
we don't

remember—
the sky
openly

swears at us
so far
we haven't judged

any of this
correctly
although our

judgment
is too corrupted
to prove it

over there
they look
exasperated

no way to leave
we dryly
conclude

better to affirm
what others
whose

needs remain
unmet
affirm

phenolic
clouds
flake

behind
colonnades
burning

sleeves
roast
kisses

immersed
in wet
skin

Nothing to Adjust

the speech
of animals

is necessity
without shape

a plain
bouncing out

of the indifferent
to sea

the object
of itself

being prepared
like nothing

before it
seductively clinging

to the frayed
bunch

thought bares
and *makes*

no regression
from privations

but takes
the time

to rejoice
if stabilized

like small rocks
in tea

it is the shed
illusion

perpetuates
the pile of candor

unbridled words
more or less

envenom
it

it meaning
what

restrains
alienation

in error
implausibly

farcical
that is

in effect
a chance

or effect
of chance

whose ludic
wings

orbit
a thick mass

that the sprout
knows not

let the hair
and so forth

be permeated
by spirits

and their
advisors

are there
sufficient

remote
contingencies

to align them
properly

organs
of speech

stroll past
without

disparaging
anyone

read somewhere
tin tongues

prolong
wickedness

memo to file
bottles clank

courtesy of
unfailing

sensitive
faculty

ground of
eternal

boilerplate
buzzing

by mistake
depart

organic
drivers

don't applaud
who blot

their own
wherewithal

untested
is their

prophetic
strength

I too
towards whom

I was not
hostile

turned hostile
towards me

the forest
itself

and the goats
of Choate

now
orthogonal

like every
other phrase

managed
a smile

streaming from
nearby

Nineveh
they flew

backwards
into the path

of a moth—
another way

to say this
the court

denies relief
which is not

something withdrawn
a hill or hillock

disappearing
the present is

prelusive
delusion

each footstep
more discreet

until none
or *do I get*

to that question
by your own terms

weren't you
an infant

spitting up
what's not—

no proposition
is anyone's

therefore
unaware

ten thousand
different

plastic
tubes

resonate
or not at all

in the twelfth
degree of Taurus

on the finger
of the heart

incurious
Caucasus

went berserk
dog walking by

people were
afraid you

meant
the opposite

nerves out
muscles in

longing to
twitch

they also
seek

who only
sleep

status
stunted

whoever
you are

think of
the big sky

plus one
on tiptoe

wheeling
lakeward

on May first
wildflowers

turn left
into the sun

unbeknownst
fallen to pieces

the freaks
of Nostradamus

stuffed
with cheese

whither they
vanish

is not—
pause

one year later
sweat

adorns
most excellent

pronoun
why boast

low clouds a-
spreading

Zeno said
go little

precepts
enjoy

your unknown
language

my notes
suggest

no reaction
moist

portraits
talking

at nightfall
river of

night
river of

unpaid
bills

suppose
one begins *to*

dissolve those
horrible powers

tape their
mouths shut

sua sponte
no cause

they say
trees leak

while the mighty
imagination

strains
for air

there's
something else

some new
propriety

laughing
and peeling off

trifles
to hang

numbers on
parsing

inlets and
coves

with skewed
tweezers

in
threefold

diaphanous
silence

meanwhile
wood stones

fire
flesh

sustain the
god with

two heads
staring down

the horses
of night

their jangling
hooves

nominally
in line

as echoes
or *self-continuance*

[of sound] *in the air*
a concept

burrowing
through archives

unchallenged
oblique

infected
erected

from
efflux of

quincunx
at Delphi

where a door
is opened

by zealots
a shining heap

of coarse
energy

also of gold
stand back

against the sky
shamefaced

who never was—
think you what

being is—
stand back

that that
other one

emerge
on the fourteenth day

from fresh
voids

spun in
pores

not well
but ill

like properties
associated

with existence
chopped up

by a driveling
stream

next quarter's
dissimilarity

to last
might loop in

a planet
as it waits for

a train
asking why

there's no priestess
but rather

who's that
head bowed

toward
the flicker

of sequacious
reasoning

or pool
of human

capital
used to compute

suspicious
amazement

in the world
below

mass
solitude

drags watery
pen

through
butter

which doesn't
sound odd

to speculative
types

a little
diffused

see Section C
next stop

Porlock
startling

inference
from horoscope

on surface
of bread

seems reasonable
to me

slow
fading

spell
of time

not
a bone

but a
vapor

4

Writing Policy

Writing folds easily in commercial contexts before it has a chance to congeal into good will, meaning its obligations run to representatives of other, unknown earths whose attentions are fixed on objects and problems unspecified or never-to-be-known, inflating small perceptions into one giant inference concerning all potentially relevant points as of the moment of their presumed relevance, subject to objection, though how do we know. Yet it does sometimes happen that something weaves its way through the grass or burrows underneath, perhaps a child who's curious to find a creature keeping its own counsel amid such confusion, wondering if this apparent self-sufficiency is only a pose adopted to manage anxieties, and if so what kind of complexity of disposition is required to maintain it so well and whose older managerial regime is being displaced, or are there other schemes—certainly there are—schemes intersecting at every angle, ready to convert hints of a future tranquility into chronic uneasiness, eyes shut but not resting until a breeze ruffles a small carnival of insights into the following exhibit. *The hairs of their heads rose as soon as they were bewitched, and when thou knowest this, along with other examples, the stealing of a spoon, the killing of a dove by a monkey, you will have understood the absurd antagonisms arising from the incorrect use of words.* In this way what substitutes for *what is* engages you beyond the planning stage and the service-level agreements. So you assemble all your thoughts in one place, deleting some, renaming others, and allowing still others the benefit of sunlight and clean air, so that for now your subterranean reserve is undisturbed, awaiting a time not far off when you become its nocturnal companion, speaking its name to darkness as you travel together along the rough track linking inside to outside. And if it turns out you're not awake, there's no harm, but rather a feeling of security in knowing that once you *are* awake you'll be able to model your relations accordingly, sending familiars out to dance in the sky. Episodes of congestion will intercede and how to deal with them is why this policy was written. I have prepared a sheet listing all twelve permutations of the Golden City. I'll sit here while you review it. Note that reason guards against surrendering more details than are absolutely necessary. At any rate the process is not to be evaluated except for its impact on the system of record; that system is of course fair game, and has been the traditional object of examination (*see comments of Scenescof*) although in recent years it has evolved into a collection of tangled, intricate accumulations out of which almost no order can be teased; nor are custom and habit effective guides to negotiating the system, as there are fewer and fewer practitioners who employ them, and none are currently available to instruct in their use; so it is only natural that simple, subsidiary access be sought, studied, and commented on. The straightforward point of entry supplied by verbs is one example of this, as perhaps also the occasional simile whose scaffolding has become so integral and attractive that it has permanently become part of the structure it serves. Using these tools, we divide Golden City into three realms: the realm of description, the realm of action, and the realm of inquiry. Each of these realms can be found existing inside its own custom-built labyrinth. Were we to superimpose these labyrinths on one another, the result would resemble a large hollowed-out sphere. Outside the sphere one may think freely about any object of thought, adorning it with enough discretionary detail to convince oneself that it properly exists; but inside is different. The cellar walls are stuffed with headless pins, provoking foul words from empty shapes who feed on dampness. They force you to set your hand to this book not to affirm it but to acknowledge the difficulties inherent in all books, should we subscribe to them, as you do by this act, which you later deny. A basket of strawberries is your compensation. For in the realm of description all concepts are reduced to a minimum number of dead signs, uncorrelated with anything. They become the bases for thematic reconstructions within the realm of inquiry. Meanwhile the realm of action falls speechless and is unable to move hand or foot. This throws everything open to interpretation, especially terms like *fairness* and *feeling,* which are closely tracked by a strange cloud that wants to eat them. A slew of issues then makes its way inside the sphere, winding down the muddy path to the lake, to pause under the willows. Of key concern is how to make the policy second nature when someone seeks something from someone else. Ideally those beside the lake can then cease *Ranting, Raving, and Raging,* or crying out that their vessels of drink have been spoiled by neighbors. Whose wishes are executed first becomes a matter of setting the right priorities, but there is no one to arbitrate. Or rather, I know dozens who would do so if they had the chance but there's a provision that forbids it—for now, that is, because it can be amended, albeit the procedure for this is fundamentally unclear, and it is likely no court will ever be persuaded to take the matter up, much less clarify or construe it, thanks to the policy's highly technical nature, meaning that by the time the court has heard an adequate explanation of its function, and the techniques and knowledge required to maintain it—and then heard the various rival explanations, some of them greatly detailed and highly tedious (but none of them pointing to the kind of adverse economic consequences that would be of interest to a court)—by such time as all these have occurred, the various parties will have long ago bitten, pricked, pinched, and choked one another to death. Thus writing is or is not an imaginary transgression. How to continue given lack of formal guidance becomes a daily question. For instance, should one stand beside oneself, and assess one's own conduct, changing it on the fly, examining it in light of new information, reversing the process when appropriate, or abruptly abandoning any notion of self-surveillance by closing one's eyes and tapping out messages to the local registry, messages whose coherence and sanity will be questioned simply for the fact that someone has attempted to transmit them, never mind whether they are ornamented beautifully or arranged correctly according to the old rules that the policy replaced, which in fact were never codified as rules, but left to play themselves out depending on the needs of those who took them up and which temptations they hoped to reduce by doing so. These are issues whose tenacity I admire. The question as to whether they can influence at this distance, with no intervening material, can't be answered without conceiving a silence in which the question can incubate. Descending through layers of ooze to observe this now becomes a duty.

Out of their dim hives people are drawn together by love and taught that love is a form of speech that never betrays. I see them waiting in line for the future. But I'm indifferent to them, and prefer instead to consider what it means to have delusions. First, a reference point must be established. Here again having a policy is helpful; that is, unless in a certain way it too might be read as a symptom. Regardless, right thinking can be learned from any number of creatures, provided the mind has been configured to handle the most delicate tasks of concept management. At night I lie on the floor and wonder if someone is available to lift me up. Everything hinges on my not being able to spot my own inadequacy.

William Fuller was raised in Barrington, Illinois, and studied literature at Lawrence University and the University of Virginia. His most recent books of poetry include *Quorum* (2012), *Hallucination* (2011), and *Watchword* (2006). He is chief fiduciary officer of the Northern Trust Company in Chicago.